GRANDMA HONEY AND THE CHILDREN OF LIGHT

GRANDMA HONEY AND THE CHILDREN OF LIGHT

Friends for Life

MARILYN KIRKESS

Marilyn Stevenson-Kirkess

CONTENTS

DEDICATION

A special thanks to Darri'n Deondre Dean, who inspired the name
Grandma Honey. At the age of 5, he said his great grandmother was
"As Sweet as Honey." Thus, the name Grandma Honey was born
and remains a tradition in my family today.

When I was eight, my mother became very ill. She said I was going to live with my grandmother in Boston who will take special care of me. I didn't want to leave home, especially my newly decorated room, but mama said I was too young to take care of myself. She smiled and said it will only be for a short time and that we will be together again very shortly.

Everyone said this was the opportunity to get to know my grandmother. They said I will like her once I get to know her. Mama said we have a lot in common and that we are both sweet and caring people by nature.

Betty Johnson is my grandmother's name. Mama said she is an elderly lady, not an old lady, and that there is a difference. At the age of sixty-five she is quite active, but she is old to me. I think she is the oldest person I've ever seen. Grandmother came to visit us about two years ago. She stayed for a whole week and said I should come to Boston and spend my entire summer vacation with her. I remember grandmother hugging me and she smelled like medicine. After she returned to Boston, I could still smell the medicine on me.

2

Grandmother lives on a street named Market. Mama said it is a sub-division where multi-cultural people live. When I asked what multi-cultural meant she said it is also where other races of people live.

Grandmother was standing at the door with a big smile when I arrived. She said I have really grown. She took the suitcase from me and we went into the house. When I spoke to her, she said, "Don't you hi grandmother me. Give me a big hug!" She laughed and hugged me for a long time. The medicine smell was gone. She smelled sweet, like the smell of cookies baking.

3

She must have had some type of grandmother instinct because she took me to my room that was up the stairs and said I needed to take a nap. She climbed the stairs faster than I did, carrying my big suitcase. She stood at the top of the stairs and said, "Come on child!" Now I know what mama meant when she said grandmother is active.

When I woke up from my nap, I found grandmother in the back yard on her knees. She was pulling weeds and watering her flowers. I have never seen such a beautiful flower garden. It was a sunny day. Butterflies were flying about and bees were visiting each flower. I saw two birds take a drink of water from a fountain. When I started chasing the butterflies she said, "Don't hurt them. They are so fragile child and also part of God's creation."

5

Grandmother was tall and round. At the age of eight I think all adults looked tall to me. She wore glasses and had round rosy cheeks. I immediately liked her silver hair which she wore pinned in the back. I remember wanting to touch it. Her skin was a soft tan and glowed when she laughed.

After breakfast grandmother spent the rest of the morning making sandwiches and cookies. She was always busy, and it seems she enjoyed doing this because she began humming a tune.

When I took an interest in the cookies she said, "Help yourself, child. Just help yourself." She put her fingertip on my nose and said I was as cute as a button. Then she began laughing and her stomach was moving up and down because of the flour she had left on my nose.

7

After grandmother placed the sandwiches and cookies in the basket, she asked if I wanted to go to the park. When I asked what we were going to the park to do she said we were having a picnic. I remember going on a picnic when I was younger. That was before daddy went up to heaven.

8

When we got to the park, several children ran towards us, yelling, "Grandma Honey! Grandma Honey!" It seemed they were waiting for her. They began hugging her legs and jumping gleefully around her, but she wasn't their grandmother. She was only my grandmother.

9

Grandmother gathered all the children around me and introduced me to everyone. "This is my granddaughter, Kathy." She laughed and her rosy cheeks glowed with happiness. She told me to shake hands with her friends. I didn't know children and grandmothers could be friends.

10

After we introduced ourselves grandmother divided us into two teams. I was on the team with Timothy who was white and Mary whose ancestors are from Ireland, Juan was Mexican and Josephine was African American. Elizabeth, Grace, John, Gary and Grandmother were on the second team. Grace was Chinese, Elizabeth was White and John was African American. Gary was the only Native American I had ever met.

11

I was surprised when grandmother grabbed the bat and said, "Let's play ball!" She hit the ball and ran so fast she was at third base before my team could find the ball. Everyone cheered her on, calling her Grandma Honey as she ran from first base, to second and then third. When Gary came to bat, Grandma Honey made the first score.

After the game was over we all gathered around Grandma Honey and cheered. The other team won the game, but I didn't feel so bad for loosing. I felt good because that was the first time I had ever played baseball and because I had discovered new friends and a grandmother I never really knew.

12

During our picnic people waved and spoke, calling her Grandma Honey. My grandmother was popular. Some parents even brought their children over while they went to take care of chores. Then Grandma Honey made an announcement, "Next year on vacation we will go to Stone Mountain Park in Georgia to the Indian Festival and Pow-Wow because Gary's ancestors are Native Americans." Now that I am part of the group, I will be going too....with mama's approval, of course.

13

Every year the group takes a trip or plans activities relevant to a child's cultural background. Two years ago they went to China because that's where Grace's ancestors are from. This year the group went to Mexico because that's where Juan's family is from. I missed those trips but I will never miss another one. In two years we will be going to Africa, because that's where Josephine's, John's and my ancestors are from. They raised money for the trips by having bake sales and games. So far, they have managed to take six trips and pay college tuition for three students.

14

I learned that Grandma Honey did lots of things for children. Mama said grandma took a special interest in children because she always wanted more children, but she was only able to have one child, and that was my mama.

Grandmother said if you want to make friends and keep those friends for life, you have to appreciate cultural differences and the value each person brings to that friendship. What better way to appreciate those cultural differences than by visiting their homeland or bringing the essence of the culture to you.

15

After we ate, everyone had a chance to talk about their families. We did math problems and encouraged one another to take a guess if we didn't know the answer. I never had so much fun. If an answer was wrong, no one laughed or made fun of you. Everyone encouraged you to try again until you got it right.

Grandma said humans are part of God's creation, just like the butterflies. She said all humans are different and we should not make fun or tease others because they are different.

16

Grandma Honey talked about her family – mostly of mama. She said she was proud of her and of me. I didn't know she loved us so much. At the time I didn't understand all that she said. I was still caught up in the marvel of the day. In those three weeks I stayed with Grandma Honey, she taught me things that would last a lifetime. Never again will I view life through such a small spectrum. Before this visit all my friends were of one race. I never knew I could have friends from so many different nationalities. Some of these friends will last a lifetime – through college and beyond.

17

It was during this visit I realized how important grandmothers are and how important it is to share common passion and friendship with other races. Through grandma's eyes the world is beautiful. She said, "The different races make up the colors of a human rainbow, and if a rainbow is beautiful and something to marvel at then how can the human race not be?"

Throughout my childhood, I spent summer breaks and holidays with my Grandma Honey.

18

The End

Grandma Honey and The Children of Light continues

their adventure continues......

Color Me Not

Rainbow of colors glowing in the light;
Where do you begin? Where do you end?
Colors so bright, colors so brilliant - Color of life color me not.
Color me white. The color of purity and cleanliness.
I am superior, I feel, and will let none appeal to me;
The world is at my feet.
The color of life colored me white.
Color me red. The sign of fire, blood and wickedness
my land has seen. My land is my home under the stars;
let no other possess it - for I have grown old and
my fruits bare not.
The color of life colored me red.
Color me black. The sign of strength, beauty and spirit.
My land has disappeared from my memory and my heritage
is dim. My spirit has always been free, but my color has not.
Color of life color me not -
The color of life colored me black.

Make friends in your school or in your neighborhood

Getting to know other people with a different background enhance your perspective on different cultures and values. You can learn to appreciate your personal values and at the same time learn the values of others. Grandma Honey believes all life has value and one life should not be put before another; that we are separated because we lack knowledge of the treasure and beauty we all hold.

You can also learn that your personal views and opinions can be broadened when you interact with others from another culture. This interaction can kinder prejudice and stamp out hatred among mankind.

Take the challenge....get to know at least one person with a different background, race or culture. Keep an open-mind and learn to appreciate your differences instead of finding fault with the person. You might be surprise to learn that the person is not that much different from you. You might just be developing a friendship for life.

Remember, Grandma Honey had a vision for the world. A world that's free of hatred. That's a huge vision – one that might be impossible I use to tell her, but let's try it anyway. Do you think we can learn to appreciate cultural differences without being judgmental of others? Can you develop a friendship with someone from a different race, a different culture or background? Do you think we can do it?

Activity Page

Can you match The Children of Light with their ancestral origin?

Kathy _____ Timothy_____ Mary _____ Juan _____ Gary _____
John _____ Elizabeth _____ Grace _____ Josephine _____

Ireland - America - China - Africa - Mexico - Europe

In what countries have you made a friend? _____

Which of these statements are true about Kathy?

_____Didn't know she can make friends with other races

_____Kathy always loved her grandmother

_____Kathy remembers going on a picnic with her father

After the picnic, which of these activities did Kathy do with her new friends?

_____They did math problems

_____They teased and made fun of each other

_____Encouraged each other

Why did Kathy go to live with her grandmother?

_____Her grandmother was sick

_____She ran away from home

_____Her mother was sick

Activity Page

Which of these quotes did Grandma Honey make?

_____Learn to appreciate cultural differences
_____Appreciate the value each person brings to the friendship
_____The different races make up the colors of a human rainbow
_____A rainbow is beautiful, how can the human race not be

How many trips did The Children of Light take with Grandma Honey?

_____10
_____6
_____1

How many students did Grandma Honey send to college?

_____15
_____10
_____3

Grandma Honey took a special interest in children because....

_____She envision a world free of hatred through our children
_____She could have only one child
_____She believes children are taught prejudice and hatred
_____She believes prejudice can be kindred among mankind

Write about your new friend

Place pictures of your new friend

In Loving Memory of Grandma Honey

Book Summary

Grandma Honey had a kind humble nature and she loved children. I remember the large meals she prepared so that every child that came to her door could get a meal. It didn't matter what race the child was. If the child was hungry, he/she was stuffed like a a bird when they left. She took food from her freezer and gave it to struggling families; she gave warm coats to children and encouraging words. From her kindness came the words, "You are as Sweet as Honey." Thus the name Grandma Honey was born.

While she lived she believed that people could do better by each other - treat each other with dignity, respect and compassion. She felt that our society needs healing and racial harmony and that every man should be measured by his talent. We, as adults, had failed and it's up to our children to make this possible. She said children are the light of the world. They represent new ideals and respect for cultural differences because they have heard and lived Grandma Honey's message - that it's okay to know other people with different skin tones, different hair, and different cultures. It's okay to develop a lasting friendship with someone from a different race, and if injustice and bigotry still exists in our current society, we must take steps to remove that injustice and find a better resting place for peace. She believed the different races make up the colors of a human rainbow and if a rainbow is beautiful and something to marvel after how can the human race not be? I took her ideas of a better society through our children and began to create a society where people learn to appreciate cultural differences.

The next story in this series is, *A New Friend Named Kailey.*

CPSIA information can be obtained
at www.ICGtesting.com
Printed in the USA
JSHW011933100522
25813JS00004B/59